The Basic Blacksmith

ISBN-13: 978-1493579105

ISBN-10: 149357910X

Iron Bee publishing,

Omaha, Nebraska

2013

Table of Contents

The Basic Blacksmith

The Blacksmith trade is an age old art form that still captures and holds the interest of many people today. The new blacksmiths come from all walks of life each for their own reason. For some it's the art of forming metal and creating something beautiful or useful. For others it's a way to connect with the past and experience what it would have been like to live and work centuries ago. For myself it's all of that. I enjoy reading about the distant history, how the blacksmiths worked with almost nothing. It is interesting to me how the blacksmith was highly valued in the medieval days because he made all of the king's weapons. They were often invited to sit at the table for a meal with their king. He was the king's engineer and held in high esteem. Contrast that with the down cast member in the community that we see in the movies. This is partly because of the industrial revolution. Prior to this villagers relied on the smith to make everything metal. After the industrial revolution the once renowned blacksmith became the repair guy, a mechanic in a dirty trade and fell out of favor. Hope came in the mid 1900's with a revival of interest in the craft. There are now clubs in every state and if you go to t internet you can find people from around the world that share the same interest and some may offer stories about being a blacksmith. It's been said that there are more blacksmiths today then there were when it was an active trade.

Many of us have become collectors of the old tools and equipment. I like to find these old relics, clean them up and get them back into the hands of new smiths who will appreciate them and practice the art and craft of blacksmithing.

Garden Decorations

In the city sometimes we have to make some concessions. Here one of my favorite blowers, a Lancaster # 40 made by Champion, sets in storage…I mean, **displays its rustic beauty as a dark vertical element surrounded with the tranquil greenery of vineyard foliage.**

By incorporating my larger tools into the garden scenes I get to keep them nearby without repercussions from the better half. Having said that, I must say she is right most of the time. I would be happy covering my backyard with a two story shop, but she and the neighborhood surely wouldn't agree. The city planning department would definitely have something to say about it as well. My wife is very understanding and encourages my exploration in my hobbies. I feel I am blessed for having someone in my life to pull back on the reins when I get too far out there with my ideas.

So, the message here is to say; use your resources well. If you got the space, great, if you don't then be creative and incorporate your equipment into your life in other ways. This may not always be met with agreement from your spouse. I once offered to set a 200 pound anvil on a short stand so it could be an end table to our couch. It was an extra one I had and I thought it would have looked good there. Didn't go over well at all, even when I offered to buff it clean and spray on a coat of clear lacquer.

Safety First

The first thing one needs to think about is keeping himself and others safe. You don't want to burn down the house or shop, you don't want to cut off any body parts and you don't want to be spending time on the burn ward at the local hospital.

Some things to get and consider in the shop;

- Eye protection. Sight is a gift, protect it.
- Ear plugs or muffs...no one wants to wear hearing aids.
- Full face shield when grinding or using the wire wheel.
- Good leather foot wear, steel toes are great when dropping heavy things.
- Wear cotton clothing, it won't melt onto you or flame up. It will burn slowly, giving you time to put it out.
- Leather apron, keeps clothes clean and privets protected more.
- Good fitting leather gloves when grinding and sanding. I hate it when my knuckle hits the grinder.
- Cotton hat, keeps me from losing more hair.
- Fire extinguisher & bucket for water and one for sand. Be ready.
- First Aid kit. Water first on a burn, dry off and use on some OTC burn spray.
- Be alert, fatigue numbs the brain and you could seriously get hurt working tired.
- No adult beverage until after you close the shop. Assuming you are old enough.
- No illicit drugs. Ever! They will destroy you. I've seen it happen many times.
- Bad Attitudes need to stay away from a shop full of dangerous objects.
- Good ventilation in the shop, PROTECT you lungs Respiratory mask if need, O_2 tanks with nasal cannula aren't sexy.
- Space to work, don't be cramped so much that you trip and fall over your work or tools.

3rd Degree Burns

It never fails that when I am in a hurry I drop my work. LET IT FALL! The metal won't get hurt, **but you will** if you tried to catch it. Many times when punching or chiseling on a red hot piece of work I have lost it and it flips over hitting my other hand and it brands me. If your burn is bigger then what a band aide will cover then you may need to seek medical advice. I have found it takes me about 3 to 4 weeks to heal a small wound if kept cover. I like to use an over the counter antibiotic ointment to help it heal. The ointment traps moisture and allows the skin cells to regenerate which reduces scaring.

With all this considered, enjoy working in the shop. Teach this to everyone that comes into the shop so you don't have to pay their medical bills. Talk with your home owner insurance provider or business insurance provider and make sure you have enough coverage for yourself and others working in the shop and the customers if they come onto your property.

Learn to be safe and practice it. Protect you back. You only got one. When lifting an anvil and other heavy items off the ground get help and/or use cribbing to move it to a higher level little bit at a time.

Be safe and blacksmith long.

Starting the Fire

Years ago, in the early morning before the smith goes to work, his apprentice gets up before him to open the shop. He would start the forge fire, top off the slack tub with water and tend to any other chores the Master Smith had set out for him. He may take advantage of the empty shop and work on some project he needed to accomplish to earn his next level of lessons.

I'm going to assume you don't have an apprentice living in the back of the shop eagerly wanting to learn the craft from you. I'm guessing you are more like the apprentice and will have to teach yourself the craft. This is how most of us have learned it. From books, the internet and other smiths in the area.

Starting a coal fire. Coal fires can be troublesome to start for a beginner. A hand full of pine needles or a pine cone, some wax, or pine sap will ignite the coal quickly. You can start it with a small wood fire using kindling like shingle wood or a wad of newspaper in the center of the fire. Or if you are in a hurry you could just squirt a load of lighter fluid on it or use a self-igniting butane torch. Now, that isn't how great grandpa would have done it. He would have used whatever he had available, most likely a small wood fire or pine needles. If the coal or coke is wet from being outside in the rain you will have to make a bigger wood fire to dry out the coal.

Here I started with dry coke and pine needles. It was up and burning, well under two minutes. The pine needles have resin in them which is flammable and they produce enough heat to ignite with coke with ease.

If you use wood it may take a little longer. When your small fire is up and going add some air from the blower and pull the coal into the sides of the wood fire. Continue to pull in coal as the fire builds until you have a pile over the wood fire and it's the coal fueling the fire and not the wood. You can pull out the wood with tongs at this time or let the wood burn out. Keep air blowing into the fire but not enough to blow the fire out. As simple as this all sounds there is a learning curve to it. Practice it often and soon you will be able to fire up your forge in minutes.

If it is new coal you are working with the impurities will need to burn off. The burning of new coal will produce a yellow smoke which is the sulfur that naturally occurs in various amounts. Don't breathe this in, it will make you sick to your stomach and maybe a headache to boot.

If you are needing an intense heat for welding it is best to build a cave out of new coal. To do this add onto a strong fire a few scoops of new coal and sprinkle it with water. This will build a crust like a volcano as the tar and oils bubble out and stick together. Try to build this with the opening of the volcano on the side that you will be placing your work.

Coked coal is coal that has had the impurities burn out of it. I like to coke up a pile of coal after each day of forging for the next day's work. Just scoop on some new coal to your fire, give it some air and walk away for a few minutes coming back to stir the fire until the pile burns clean. Then scoop the coke out of the fire pit to cool. When cooled off cover it if you're working outdoors or put into a metal bucket and save it for the next burn. Remove the clinker and it's ready for the next day's work.

To identify coke, notice the shiny look of the new coal compare it to coked coals "Charcoal Gray" look. Coke is also lighter in weight due to loss of the oils in the coal. After the burn, when the forging is done, look in the bottom of the fire and you will find CLINKERS or some call them CINDERS. These clinkers were robbing you of heat. They form from the metals and other impurities trapped in the coal from its creation millions of years ago. They fuse together and take up space in your fire. While forging occasionally look into your fire. Compared to the yellow/orange glow of the burning coal, clinkers will be black spots in the fire. They

offer no heat and take up space in the fire pot making your burning area smaller. You can clean your fire up with a set of long thin tongs. Reach in, pinch and pull out the clinkers. Pack the fire with more coke or coal and
add some air from your blower.

Coal Coke Clinker

A simple display of coal, coke and clinkers can be very educational to the young on lookers. It seems in this area the 4th and 5th graders are just learning of geology and are very interested in the topic if you include stories about the coal being around before the time of the dinosaurs.

When I go to fairs and demonstrate the craft I bring the

coal in a wooden box. It makes it easier to transport. Below is the coal box in the center, a bag of lump charcoal that is sold

locally here and a 50 pound bag of coal that can be bought through clubs or the internet.

Coal is fossilized carbon. The hard form is best to use for forging and is called anthracite. Lignite, or brown coal, is the lowest ranking coal. There is a lot of variation in coal sue to its different sources. So when you find a good source keep it. Coal came from many different time periods and plant life. It was formed from sea algae in some areas, moss bogs and trees in others. Each type having its own unique properties.

Colors of Heat

When working with steel it is important to work the metal in the proper heat range. If you strike it too cold it will crack and if it's left in the fire too long it will burn. Starting with a cold piece of steel the color is black. It will stay black as the heat increases until it passes about 1000° F. The colors of temperature will be a little different for each person and each shop setting. Because our perception is different from one person to the next and if you are outside in the sun you won't see the cherry red heat color until the metal is much hotter compared to working inside where the lights are dim. In general the colors and heat ranges are as follows, and please keep in mind that everyone sees colors a little differently so practice is the key.

Sparkling like the 4th of July	2500 >
White Hot	2500
Bright yellow	2400
Medium Yellow	2300
Dark Yellow	2200
Light Orange	2000
Medium Orange	1800
Dark Orange	1600
Light Red	1400
Medium Red	1200
Cherry Red	1100
Black	1000 and <

When to work the metal

Dark red can be hammered on with some difficulty. Can be hot filed with an old wood rasp. Working carbon steel at the lower temps will cause cracks.

Cherry red it is more malleable, you can work steel and quench higher carbon steel for hardness. Be aware when working thin metal you will lose this heat fast.

Orange Heat is good for most work. At this heat you can hammer, punch, chisel and upset the work without worry until it cools back to the dark red, then it's time to go back into the fire.

Yellow Heat Is my favorite temp to work in when drawing out or just working the metal in general. The heat lasts a little longer as it cools to a dark red and give me time to think about what I'm doing.
Welding Heat is sometimes call yellow-white or white heat. While in the fire be careful not to be distracted at this point it is easy to start talking or thinking of your next step and let the metal burn.

Welding Heat The optimum temp for welding is around 2500 degrees. You want the surface to be molten but not bubbling and sizzling as in burning the steel. Try to keep the work out of direct blast of air from your blower. This will help minimize the burning.

Too Hot. If you create a 4th of July Sparkler out of your metal and pieces are falling off, it has been ruined and it's time to start over.

Here is a good example of black heat going to cherry red to a light red. This picture was taken in the evening and outside, if it was during the day or inside your shop, you may see it as black to dark red.

Take your time in working a project. Strike it when it's hot and then reheat as often as needed. The consequence is cracked steel and then you have to start over. As old Ben said, (Benjamin Franklin) 'Take time for all things: great haste makes great waste. Prior to him, in about 1575 was some unknown author who said, 'Haste makes waste, and waste makes want, and want makes strife between the good man and his wife.

So, we should be frugal in our use of time, energy and resources.

Moving the Metal

Metal is move and shaped from the impact of our tools. We heat the work to make it malleable and this keeps the material from having stress cracks and breaking before you get it done. Work it only when it is red hot or hotter. We all get in a hurry at times but this proves to take more time because the work cracks or breaks and we have to start the project over. The old adage of do it right the first time applies well here.

Sir Isaac Newton, gave us some laws of physics to think about. His third law states roughly "for every action there is an equal and opposite reaction."

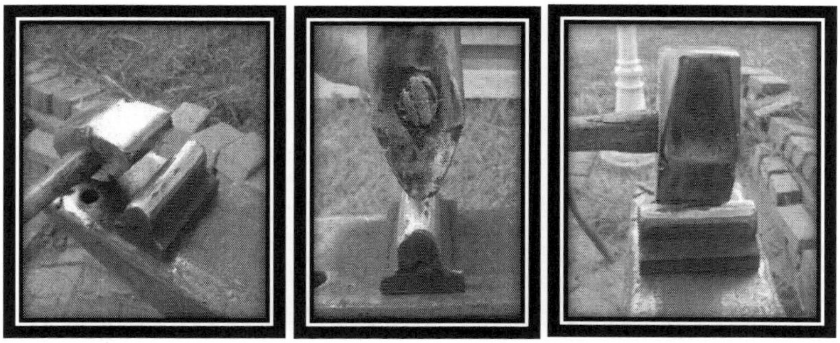

Bottom fuller with matching straight peen. This will move the metal to the right and left of the hammer.

So, what can we take away from that you might ask? When you strike the hammer on your work over the anvil, the impact is met by the anvil as it pushes back on to your work from the bottom in an equal amount of energy. This may be true in theory but if you have a soft cast iron anvil the force of the opposite reaction is dissipated into the soft anvil.

If you have a good quality steel anvil it will work. To find out if an anvil is good or not let your hammer tell you. Strike it in the center with the flat face of a hammer one time. It should give out a sharp ring, a "Ping!" and the hammer should bounce high off from the anvil. Try this on a cheap imported anvil made of soft cast iron and the sound will be a definite thud. This poor lump of metal, I mean anvil just took the energy out of your hammer, absorbed it, and giving nothing back. It is fun to refer to these as ALO's "Anvil Like Objects" and boat anchors. My advice is to buy quality if you can, if the option isn't presenting itself, buy the cheap one and keep looking for a better one.

A good anvil will push back. Use this to your advantage. If you choose a straight peen hammer and you hold the work over the edge of the anvil or on the horn, your work will received an impact in the same shape on both sides. You could use a hardy fuller or swage to get the same effect. Use one that matches the shape of the hammer or use a top fuller or swage with its own handle. This will give you the quickest results of moving the metal.

In the case of using a straight peen over a matching fuller, the metal will move to the left and right of the hammer peen. If you use a round peen it will cause the metal to move in all directions. The cross peen will move the metal forward and backward from the peen. The flat face of the hammers and sledges will push the metal inward, as well as, outward in all directions. To smooth out the dimples and ridges us a flatter in conjunction with a sledge hammer. After you have shaped the work, heat and place the flatter on it then strike the back of the flatter. It works best to have a helper strike the blow so you can concentrate on tool control. Repeat as needed. Don't use the flatter as a hammer, it's not a hammer.

Tools

The tools use by the Smith are simple in nature but specific to each task. The hammer and anvil are icons for blacksmithing. Usually the image is a hammer, anvil and a big muscular guy pounding away on it. The fact is many smiths weren't that burly and a lot of times it was the wife and kids of the smith that worked in the shop doing the repetitive jobs like making nails, rivet and bolts. The children worked to help make an income for the family. The eldest was often expected to take over so he would be working as apprentice for many years.

The pictures in this book are some of my tools I have collected over the years. Some are over 100 years old and still good and functional as the day they were made. Try comparing that track record with some of today's tools like computers. The one I am writing on was obsolete the day I bought it from the discount store, that's why it was on sale.

Soon it will break down and get recycled for the little bit of metals in it. In a 100 years... will anybody care?

HARDIES

Twisting hardy, sq. block with partly smooth edge for fullering inside bends so they don't crack, cold and hot cut off hardies, small round cone, large fuller, V swage, shoulder hardy, Veining hardy for leafs and in the center is a double fuller or guillotine.

Hardy tools are used to create specific shapes in the metal. On the tail of your anvil you will find a square hole. This is referred to as the hardy hole and is made to hold these small tools called hardies. The can make grooves, raised bumps, various designs and shapes, as well as, cutting, and stretching metal in a circle. They are also useful in scrolling, bending and folding the metal.

The Cut off Hardy and Chisels

The Hardy Chisel is the most common and well known tool for your anvil. If you have to buy your tools this one a

smith must have. This chisel drops into the Hardy Hole and provides a quick and easy way to cut steel to length or to cut off excess steel. There are two straight cutting edge forms of the Hardy chisel: one for cutting steel cold and one for hot cutting. The cold cutting Hardy chisel is much heavier a structure so to stand up to heavy blows when cut into cold hard steel. The hot cut on the other hand has a thinner cutting edge and is designed to cut rapidly into hot metal. There is a curved one, often used by the farrier when making a horse shoe and cutting off the ends as a half rounded end.

Cold Hot

To the right are a pair of hot and cold chisels on handles. The thicker one on the left is for cutting cold steel. The one on the right is for cutting hot steel. In practice the smith will have to use a hold down for securing his work and hold a chisel in one hand and a hammer in the other. Here is where an apprentice would come in handy.

Bending Tools

Scroll work may be a big part of what will be made in your shop.

These bending tools are great for twisting stock. A twist can make a handle or decorative piece in a sign or railing. The one on the left is a fixed twisting wrench. It will fit 1/4" square stock and be helpful on adjusting scroll work.

The old style adjustable end wrench that is painted red is my favorite to use because it will fit any size that I will be working on. I welded on an eight inch shaft to the head to give a balanced pressure while I twist a square shaft.

This hardy tool is a great help in scrolling and creating uniform loops on handles. The round shaft on the right is a piece of one inch stock. The piece on the left is notched to catch and hold the work. The bottom is for ¼" the next is $^{3}/_{8}$'s and the top is for bending ½"heated stock.

The 2 prong hardy is slightly limited in the size it will

work with, but they are easy to make in different sizes.

Anvils

On the Fourth of July Grandfather, like many smiths,

would blow an anvil to start the festivities. This would entail taking 2 anvils out to an open field, placing the larger one upside down on the ground. Then take a ball of clay, work it into a long rope and place it on the inverted bottom of the anvil in a large oval ring. Most anvils have a cavity on the bottom. This is filled with black powder, a fuse installed, and the other anvil is placed right side up over the powder load and clay seal. When the time was right the fuse would be lit and all would surly run like … well, run real fast away from there. The resulting boom would rattle the window through the town and signal the start of the celebration.

There are many styles of anvils. These are a few I have to play with. The bottom 2 are of the Trenton brand, the bottom is a 225 pounder, second one weighs in at 200 lbs., the 3rd one up is a 140 lbs. B.I.C. Omaha, 4th is a 80 lbs. Vulcan, then to top it off is a little 10 pounder I use it in my Wee Smithy display of miniature blacksmith tools.

Anvils are GREAT to have around and so useful. You can blast them into the air, drop them from tall buildings, and devise ways to smash fast running desert birds. Everyone should have a good anvil.

Cutting Plate

The anvil is an important tool in the shop and care should be taken to preserve it. Make a cutting plate that will cover the working face of the anvil. When cutting through a piece hot of steel it often happens that you cut through and damage you tools. Mostly it will be the cutting chisel that is damaged but the face of the anvil will also take some abuse. Make a cutting plate this out of mild steel flat plate 5" X width of the anvil. Give it a 1" lip on 2 sides so not to jump off while you're working on it.

Another version is to have a mild steel plate welded onto a square shank that fits into your hardy hole.

Post Vise

On the outside of my shop I have a set up for coal forging. Below is pictured a 6.25" post vise and below that is a little 4" that I take out on demonstrations. I have another 6" mounted on my work bench inside the shop. These vises

were made to take a beating. They were bolted to a heavy wood bench and then anchored into the concrete floor or on a stone base. It is common to find 4" to $6^{1/4}$" wide jaw post

vises still in use today. They are a work horse in the shop that have proven themselves to be valuable over the years.

This little 4" is mounted on a saw horse type stand for demos. The bottom line is get the heaviest one you can find and anchor it well to your work bench or as I did to a railroad tie sunk in the ground. There is little to go wrong with them, check the spring in the middle. Make sure it isn't broke, if it is...well you are now a blacksmith, make one. Leaf spring from a car is a good source of material.

This was Grandpa Arthur Tuttle's vice.

His 6" vise is holding my barrier stakes used to define my area around a demonstration site and keep the kids safely at a distance.

I remember cranking on this vise when I was about 8 or 9 years old. I made the mistake of letting the shaft slide with my hand still hanging onto it. Oh, what a pinch it did make, giving me a heck of a blood blister. It took a few reminders, but I eventually learned to let go of the handle and let it slide on its own.

Post Drill Press

This is a small hand cranked Buffalo Post Drill that I use in my demonstration. It is mounted on a 4"X4" post and secured to my saw horse that holds my anvil and post vise. It is functional but I bring it mostly for show.

Many Post Drill styles and sizes were made over the years. Some with had cranks and some with hand wheels to be turned. Each have a mechanical advancing mechanism so you, in theory, only have to turn the crank. Many had flat pulleys so as to be driven by a belt from the line shaft.

This one has both a flat pulley with a “V” belt grove cut into it to be powered by a modern electric motor.

Two views of a hand powered drill.

It is a shame that so many of these beauties have been

scrapped. If you have one you can't use then you might consider making it into a mail box holder or a yard decoration. If set up on a post in the yard it could display to the public your blacksmith business sign.

Swage Block

15" X 15" X 4" Swage Block

The cousin to the Anvil is the Swage Block. It was used to help bend, cut and form shapes in the metal. Commonly they have half circles, V shapes, half of a hexagon shapes, and internal shapes to allow the smith many

options to work with. Corresponding swage shapes mounted on a handle were available. These were needed when working a shaft into the shape desired. The size of each block varied from one manufacturer to another. They commonly were about 4" wide and 15" square, but could be larger or smaller and rectangle as well. The better ones were made of steel and could take more abuse over the years. Cheaper ones were cast iron and would crack if struck wrong. Many of these cast iron ones were the first to find their way to the scrap yard.

Line Shaft

The line shaft is the equivalent to your extension cord that you used today in the shop. It was a way to

transfer energy. Outside the shop was a power source. It was a Steam Engine, a Hit and Miss Engine, a Water Wheel or in some parts of the world, a Wind Mill, an animal walking a tread mill or a walk around. These sources of power delivered a mechanical energy that was brought in by a heavy shaft then stepped down to lighter shaft lines that ran along the ceiling of the shop. The shafts had pulleys of various sizes on them. They were positioned above the machine to be powered. Some machines required more speed or less and an additional shaft with pulleys was needed to create the step up in speed or power. These were the transmissions of the day. The even had shifters. Some were elaborate lever systems that moved a belt form one pulley to another. Some systems simply used a stick to kick off the belt or help the belt catch the edge of the pulley and let it walk its way on.

ACME

I have always wondered if there was really an ACME company that one could mail order an anvil from. The

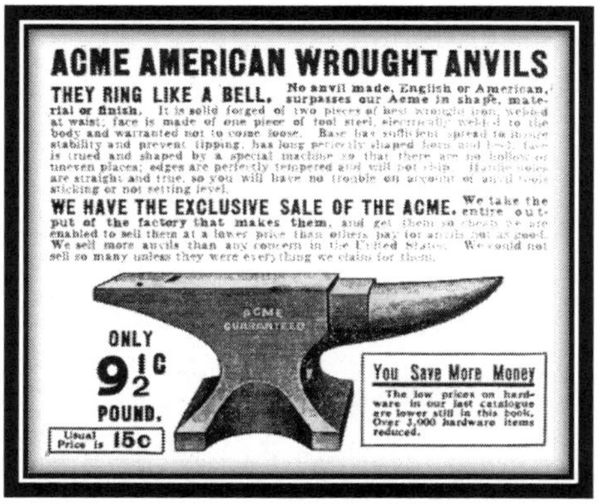

answer is yes, but, I doubt if a coyote could really get one delivered very quickly to a remote desert location.

Wish I could buy one at this price now.

Grinder

Stone wheels have been used for centuries to sharpen blades and tools. They were powered by hand cranks, treadle or peddles or a belt from a line shaft. Prior to them was a stationary stone and the workman had to do all the moving. This was certainly a slower tedious process, aren't you glad

we have moved past that stage.

Hammers

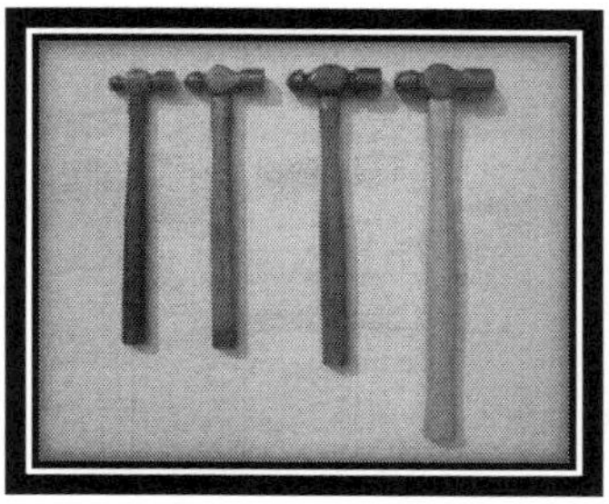

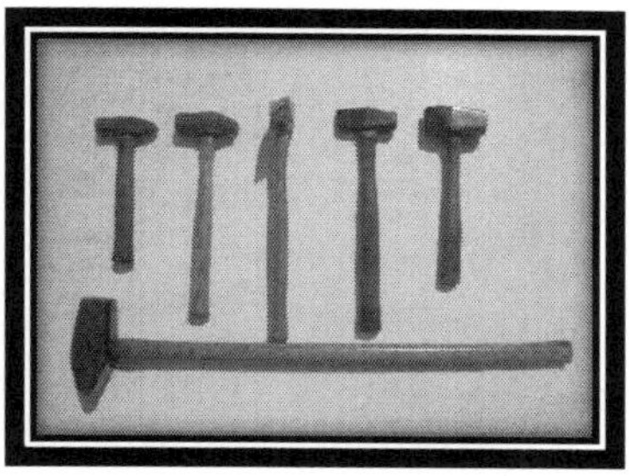

Ball Peens 3 cross peens, diagonal peen, 2 straight peens

Hammers are not just simply a stick with a hunk of metal on it. They come in many styles, each developed in their own region of the world. The French, the German, the Swedes, to name a few, all had their own style of hammers. I will be discussing the peens mostly. The hammers are grouped as sledge, peen, and specialty hammers. Many smiths make their own hammers with head that leave a texture on the work. This is often used to make a tree bark effect on branches. The sledge is the work horse of the group. It is just a simple block of steel weight on a stick made to move metal quick or to drive other tools.

There are two faces to most hammers, the flat working face and the peen. The shape of the peen determines which direction the metal being worked will move. If you hold the handle of a straight peen in your hand, the shape of the peen will be in line with the handle. When struck the metal will be forced to the right and left of the handle. The cross peens edge runs 90 deg. to the handle and will move the metal forward and backward in relationship to the handle. The ball peen moves the metal in all directions and leaves a round dimple in the work. This is the texture some people want to see and expect from hand forged work. A less common peen is the diagonal peen. Diagonals comes in a right and left angle type. These are more comfortable to use in many instances like when holding the metal work in your left hand, resting the work on the anvil, and striking it with your hammer in the right hand. The diagonal peen is more ergonomic and allows the smith to deliver more power with each blow to his work because he doesn't have to get into an awkward position and loose the leverage and power.

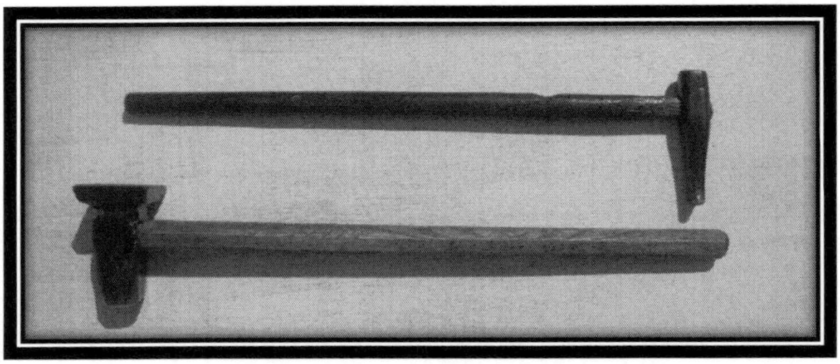

Specialties tools, on top is a hand held top fuller, on the bottom is a Flattener.

The top fuller is often held by the smith while the assistant strikes the top of it. If you have your work secured with a hold down on your anvil you could manage the fuller and striking hammer. The flattener is used to smooth out the surface of your work. Place it over the hot work and strike and move half way down the work and strike again. Do this so not to create edges on you work.

Punches and Chisels

2 Cold chisels, hot cutting chisel, 2 round punches, my Anvil punch, larger round punch, sq. punch, small rivet set that I use to make eyes on faces, Cutting chisel for making hammer head, round drift punch and an old bending tool.

Punches and chisels come in a multitude of shapes, sizes and purpose. They are used to mark the metal, to shape it and to make cuts or remove metal and to put your companies mark on it.

Making Faces

One great practice is to pound a face into a rail road spike or ¾ inch square stock.

You will use a sharp straight chisel for most of the defining work like cutting the mustache, the mouth, eye brows, nose and a blunt straight chisel is then used for some softer marks creating a more sculptured look. The use of a rounded edge square or rectangle punch to push back the hot metal into the stock. This is to bring out the other features like a nose, lips, or eye brows. The round punch can create the orbital if the eye. Follow this with an eye set punch that you will have to make as well.

Making the eye set punch is done by using a round tapered punch with a flat tip. Heat this and drive it onto a small cold ball bearing. To help not shoot the ball bearing across the room, drill a shallow dimple into a piece of steel, clamp it into the vise, set the ball bearing in it then center the hot punch on it and strike the punch just once. Check to see if you made the impression that you want. You may have to repeat this to get it right. If the tip bends reheat and hammer it straight again and continue. It's acceptable if the new impression is not centered, you can grind away the extra thickness from one side to make a even rim around the half sphere you just pushed into the point of you new tool.

Create the eyes in your work prior to creating the eye brows. With your blunt rectangle punch heat your work and move the eye brows down a little over the eyes. This can give your face a little attitude.

At last, using the sharp chisel again cut little marks to represent hairs of the beard, mustache and eye brows.

Pritchel

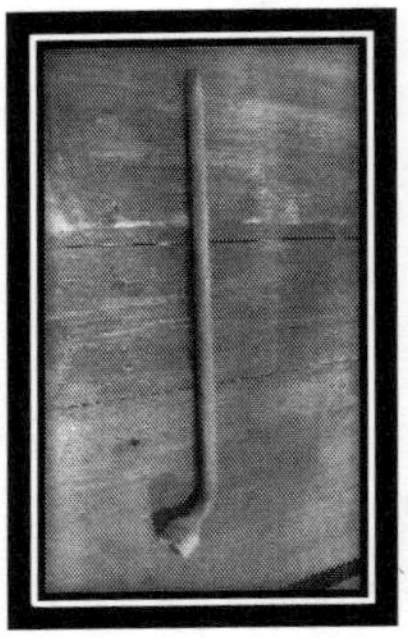

A pritchel is a type of punch used in forging horse shoes. It is a tool that makes a special hole in the shoe for the horse shoe nail. The Pritchel hole is a small round hole on the tail of most anvils. When punching through a piece of metal it is done over this little hole to gain the best support and clearance for the tool to pass. If the work is done over the Hardy hole the edges will curl down and it deforms the work. Both of these holes are often used with a hold down tool.

Tongs

Tongs come in many shapes and styles.

The basic tongs are straight lip tongs, closed or opened for holding flat work and the concave lip for holding round stock or pipe. Often you will see pictures of a blacksmith shop

with a wall covered with tongs hanging in rows. That is because, as it seems, for every job there needs to be a special set of tongs to hold the work properly. Imagine, after a few years there could be a lot of special tools on your wall as well.

Hold Downs

Dog leg hold down pictured above, gets the hold down out of your way so you can strike your work with less chance of hitting the hold down. Concave foot grips round items better, this one

has a straight shaft but could be of a dog leg design.

The hold down tool generally has a straight end that inserts into the Pritchel hole, arches up and over to the face of the anvil ending with a flattened foot that is used to hold your metal work firmly in place freeing up the smiths left hand to hold other tools.

You can make one of these out of cold rolled round stock or something better. Just bend as you see it in the pictures and

try it out. The foot may have to be concave or flattened with groves cut into it with a chisel for grip.

Learning from Others

The best way for a person to learn is different for each one of us. We learn by reading, watching, hearing, and/or doing. Then the setting matters as well. Some learn better with one-on-one lessons. Others thrive in a group setting with input from the others. Find your best way to learn and enjoy it. Some people benefit from writing notes in a note pad others might do well from drawing pictures. I do a little of both when I'm out learning from others. I draw the picture and make notes on the topic. At times if I remembered to bring my camera I'll take a photo of the item being made.

Books offer a tangible reference. They will sit on the shelf and wait for you or will accompany you in the shop as you work. Static pictures to look at can be a great help when trying to duplicate a project. To many of the younger smiths books are antiquated, but I feel they have their place. Can you picture a shop filled with smoke and dust from metal work and having a nice laptop open to look at pictures? Not going to work out well. As you work, frequently there will be hot sparks flying across the room. Crunchy keys and cinder burned screens are expensive to repair.

In the right setting the internet is invaluable. I enjoy learning from the many smiths from their websites, on You Tube and Facebook. I like watching the people in other countries showing off their blacksmith techniques. Join a local blacksmith association. The Artist **Blacksmith's Association** of North **America** is the most distinguished **blacksmith** organization. It has members from all around the world, who come together in their conferences to teach, share and support the members. Get out and practice.

Projects

When I first started I got the equipment set up, bought my coal and set fire to it. I was ready, except I didn't have a clue of what to make. I had seen awesome stuff that people had made but how do I get there? I found that I had a great ability to make metal flat, bent or lumpy, but not much else. Here I have included several projects that allow you to practice the skills needed to move the metal and create usable items. Each basic skill is used by smiths every day in their larger projects so practice them and engage your imagination.

Moonshine Mug

To make this handle start with 8 inches of 1”x1/8” steel. Make a cut in the one end, down the center about 3 inches. You could use a hack saw or heat and chisel the cut. If chiseling is your chosen option, heat and place it on a cutting plate on top of your anvil. Hold it in place with a flat foot hold down bar. Use a sharp chisel and when you have lost your heat don't forget to dip the chisel into the slack tub and cool it off, the edge will last longer.

After the cut is done, heat the metal and work these two strips down in a 90 deg. angle from each other to form a "T". Continue working them to a square point then put a little scroll on each one. Reheat and bend the two points into a large "U" shape and adjust it to snugly fit onto a mason pint jar. Use a caliper and take a reading of the diameter of the Mason jar. Find that diameter on you anvils horn. Mark this spot in white chalk and use this spot to shape the U. remember the handle needs to slip straight onto the glass jar and not wrap around.

If you are planning to make several of these it will be a great help to get a steel pipe the same size as the neck of the Mason jar. Use this to adjust the U shaped fork while hot.

Cut off about 2 inches of a heavy wall pipe and make one cut into it. Now you can open it up to the right size or cut out more and close it to the correct size, depending on if your starting pipe dimension is larger or smaller than the Mason jar. Form this into a U shape. Now you could put it the vise as it is or weld it to a hardy stub and use it on your anvil.

The other end of the handle can be tapered to a rounded point then and rolled up. Another option is put a taper in the middle to a slight hour glass shape and a fish tail on the end. The fish tail is achieved by heating the end and with a cross peen striking the end purposely leaving marks

and spreading out end like a fish tail.

Left to right, Stages of making the Moonshine Mug Handle

Another decoration is the use a sharp chisel and carefully put four diagonal marks up the center then four more diagonal marks going the other direction and making perfect X's on your handle.

Now that the decorative marks are in place reheat the piece and bend to desired shape. The general shape should be a pleasing curve coming out from the top and turning down to the bottom fishtail scroll.

An option for the center markings is to add chisel markings in the shape of a U up the center of the handle to make a pattern of fish scales or use a ball peen hammer and put dimples evenly all over it for texture. This will add value and help your product sell at a higher price. See how to make a fish scale chisel in "Making Tools."

When making sales at a demonstration, a little humor goes a long way in making the deal. You might try this line and make up others. The more pieces of humor you have prepared and rehearsed the more fun you'll have.

"Put a Handle on your Mason Jar of White Lighting, and you'll be sipping Shine in style, unless you are too young or it's a Sunday then a Sarsaparilla is in order,... with a scoop of ice cream."

If your product looks good and the customer is laughing along with you then the sale is helped. If they don't get the joke then you may want to change you approach.

S Hook

The S hook is commonly used in camp sites of the reenactment groups, campers, and folks who want to decorate their fireplaces at home with authentic items hand made by a blacksmith.

Start with 1/4" square stock. Cut to length about 10" to 12" long, hang onto it with tongs and heat one end. If it was heavier material you can use a straight peen and draw out to a point. But with this size it works well with the flat head. Work it down as a square to a point. Heat the point and hammer it over the edge of your anvil then turn it over and continue to roll the point up. Heat about 4" of the end and with the new rolled end set it over the horn and tap it around in a semi-circle to make one end of the hook. Now repeat on

the other end with the curl coming to the same side. Heat again in focusing on the middle. Place it in the vise so the middle is hanging out and with your tongs twist one and a half turns, ending with an S shape. To correct any crookedness in the twist, don't use a steel hammer. Set it on a block of wood and hit it with another piece of wood. This is done so you don't damage the ridges on you twist.

Another item to make and sell is the Tree Hook. It is a simple variation of the S hook. Just make the twist closer to one end and make a fold back like the one in the picture above so it can be hammered into a tree.

Folded Leaf Key Rings

Every leaf turns out a little different. The single leaf above stayed in the fire too long and got its tip burned off. I thought it was shot, but it just made it look more real.

Start with a 3/8" round rod. Heat and forge a point. Hold over the edge of the anvil at about 1 $^{1}/_{4}$" from the point. Strike making an impression on the anvil side. Rotate a quarter turn and strike again. Continue narrowing the stock away from there. Thin it to about an $^{1}/_{8}$" thickness. This will become the stem. Heat the point and smash flat, making a crude leaf shape. Now fold over by placing the leaf in the step of the anvil and striking at the center with a straight peen. Continue to fold over making a tight fold at the center. Re-heat and place in vise, using a chisel, catch the edge of one side and re-open the leaf. Don't open it completely and remember no 2 leaves are alike. After it is open you can dress up the edges then turn your attention to the stem. Give yourself 1$^{1}/_{2}$" to 2" and cut off. Smooth up the cut then reheat. Bend the stem around making a loop big enough to except a key ring. Clean and finish.

Many tree leaves are serrated. If you want this look, place the leaf in the vise and make little starter cuts with a hack saw then follow up with a triangular file. Make each file cut so the serrated points all flow towards the point of the leaf. After you are done filing reheat and quench to get the gray blue color on the filed areas.

The Process of making a leaf isn't too much different from making a spoon. On a six inch piece of 3/8" round you could make a leaf on one end then turn it around and make a spoon on the other end. The center could have a square area and twisted. To make a spoon just don't point the tip as when making a leaf, focus on creating width and roundness. You may want to shape it a little on the grinder. Then if you have a swage block with a concave shape use this to shape your spoon. If not, make a swage in the end of a log or post. To do this heat up a piece of round stock and burn the impression into the wood ad scrape out the chard wood leaving the hard wood to become your new swage. If it isn't yet right, use a ball peen hammer and finish it by pounding the wood into the shape you want.

Knotty Key Rings

A knot tied in steel on a key ring is easy and quick to make. Taper one end of a 2' piece of 1/4" round stock then heat and bend over about 3" leaving a gap of at least 1/2" and then re-heat. Using 2 sets of tongs grab and bend the end around the main stock and try to point it into the newly formed hole. Reheat and continue tapping, pushing and pulling the point around the main stock and through the hole. Reheat again and tap with a small hammer in the direction of the material forming the knot and tightening it up. When tight cut off the short end, hammer back the sharp edges and file smooth. On the other end, taper and bend into a loop for a key ring. If you draw out the end for the loop long enough you can wrap the point around itself giving it a rope feel and look. Or flatten the end that will receive a key ring and punch a hole through it. Then file smooth and finish as desired. Putting a colored ring on it adds a little sparkle to it.

Another variation and good practice is to give the stock an organic look to it before you tie it into a knot. Start with round or square stock and hammer it into a rough octagonal shape. Heat the whole area that you will be using for your knot and pinch one end in your vise. Using tongs or an adjustable end wrench, twist a couple of times. Now you should have a piece that looks a lot like a grape vine. Continue making your knot and plan to sell this for a little more for your effort.

Other knots are possible. If you are a fisherman, try making a knot for a fish hook or the Hangman's noose a square knot or a bow tie.

How about a Christmas present idea is to cut off a piece of 3"x3" square tubing. Make it 3" long so you have a square. Weld in a bottom and top. Then wrap a $^{3}/_{8}$" strip around the top to simulate a lid that slides over the top of the box. With this size of present you could tie with 10 gage copper wire. With larger ones you might try ¼" rod or ¼" x $^{1}/_{16}$" flat straps.

Ribbons for the Ladies

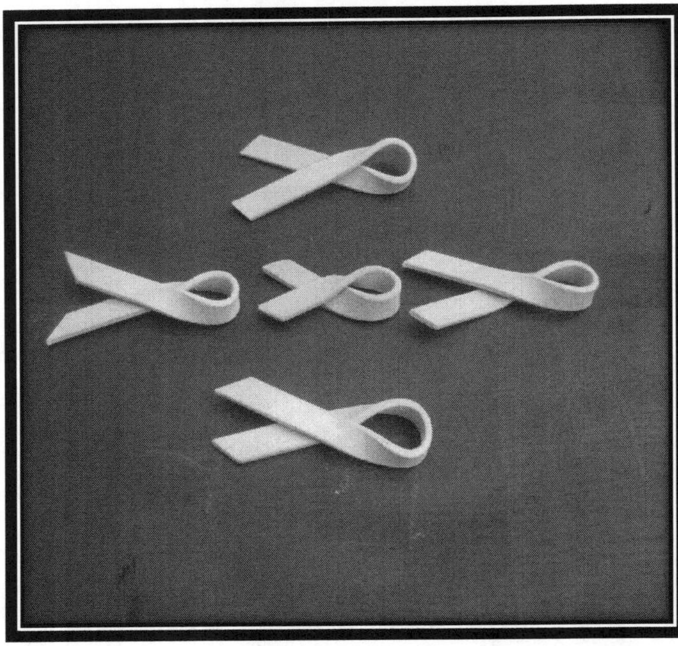

1/8" X 1/2" flat bar bent, twisted and painted Pink

NOT FORSALE

Each day at the fairs I make a handful of these ribbons but haven't sold one yet. I don't intend to sell them. I make these to give the cancer survivors or family members that have suffered with cancer. Many times ladies will come by my demo display wearing a pink shirt or a hat with a ribbon on it. I ask if they know anyone that has cancer or was a survivor, and they usually do. Many times it is themselves. I then offer them one for free. Their face lights up with a big smile, that's payment enough for me.

Cut an 8" long piece of 1/8"x1/2" flat bar with sharp diagonals so the points are both on the same side. I take of any sharp edges and points with a file then bend in half or wrap around a 3/4" diameter shaft. I can do this without any heat. Now you should have a U shape. Place the bottom of the U in the vise and using an adjustable end wrench or the tongs twist the upright points ¼ turn in opposite directions. Now place a backup hammer on the side of one point and strike the other causing them to come together and cross making the ribbon look. Brush clean and spray paint with a light pink.

One lady surprised me with a new idea for the pink ribbon made of steel. She put it on her key chain and said she would use it as a weapon if she was ever attacked.

Wee Smithy

This is an ongoing project of mine. I call it Wee Smithy because if its size. The anvil is about 7" long and I use it to base the scale of the tools on. I plan to add more tools to the collection as time permits.

Leaf Door Pull

Make a decorative door pull out of a ½ inch round stock tailored to your hand or your customers hand. To figure the length needed to make the door pull measure your hand or the customers across the knuckles and add a 1/2 inch for ease of access for the hand. Add 1 inch for each side and another 1 1/2 inch for each leaf.

Draw each end to a blunt point. Heat and hang over the edge of the anvil at about a 1.25 inch and forge a grove all away around the shaft. Flatten the pointed end to form the leaf shape. Use the cross peen to put some veining texture on them then use a center punch to make a mark for drilling a hole for the nail or bolt that will hold the handle on. If you want you can use a flat point punch to punch a hole instead of drilling. After the leaf is done heat and place the leaf on a flat piece of mild steel. This is to protect your punch and the face of the anvil. While hot strike to make your punch mark then turn over the work and center the punch on the flatten mark left on the work. You may have to flip the leaf one or more times and slide it over the Pritchel hole or hardy hole to punch all the way through. Now heat and use the square drift punch to make a square hole for a carriage bolt or leave it round for a nail.

Demonstrating Your Craft

At a Fair or other demonstration venues there is limited space. If you set up a table (and you should) decorate it with items of different sizes, different prices categories and add color, it will be more attractive to your customers. It

would be awesome if you could add smells and sound that are pleasant and relevant to your work. Think of the stores that you go to. If they were decorated in rusty brown and black it would look drab and uninviting, sales would go down. Generally the only smell the blacksmith makes is the smelly sulfur smoke. Many people come and share how they knew I was here at the fair before they saw me. They would say, "When I was young we burned coal. The memory of the smell never goes away."

If you are in a situation where the coal smell is a big problem, change to Lump Charcoal. It will smell better. The down side of burning Lump Charcoal is that it burns up quicker then coal and it snaps and pops shooting little cinder and ash out of the fire. I lost a nice canvas covered bellows because of this. A better and proper covering for a bellows it a thin pliable leather. But there is a cost factor…and it directed me to use the cheap canvas.

On the table I set out Moonshine mugs on a colored handkerchief. Most of the ladies and some of the gents stop over and examine them. Some by a single mug some will buy a set of 4. One fellow smith picked up a job of making several for a wedding party.

To stimulate the customers imagination add the sparkel. Fill one of the jars with colored marbles, one with a wax candle

and one with flowers. You could use one as your personal

water mug and tease about having very weak Moon Shine in the Mason jar.

Hanging items like dinner bells and wind chimes catches the eye. I make the traditional dinner bell, a treble clef bell and apple shaped bells. The apple bells have a green leaf on the top and the rest is painted red. I also make and sell garden hooks. They are pushed into the ground and pots of plants are hung from them. Except I hang the dinner bells from them.

Making Tools

Fish Scale Chisel

To make a fish scale chisel select a chisel about $^5/_8$" to $^3/_4$" wide, anneal it by heating it to a red heat, and let it cool in some sand, ash or dirt.

First hammer it flat and have all of the taper on one side. Then using a swage and thin cross peen, shape into a U. Let cool and then do any clean up you might need to do. Grind on the outside of the U shape to get a smooth uniform shape, use a round file on the inside of the U to clean it out. Then reheat to a cherry red and quench in oil.

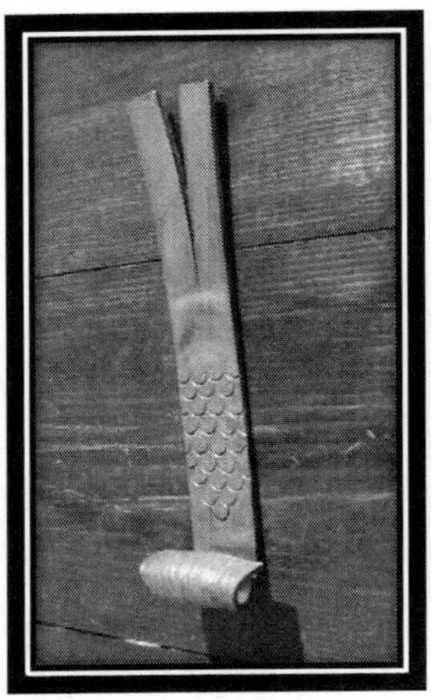

Fish Fin Scroll and Scales

Here is one use of the fish scale punch, this could be used on an item in the shape of a dragon or the siding of a Victorian style of a house. It could be a cut out in 14gage steel with chisel marks making the windows and siding. Then Paint it like the old Painted Ladies (Victorian homes were often painted in white and trimmed in 3 to 4 shades of lavender to burgundy.

A dragon shape cut out of 14ga. steel then textured with scales and chisel marks would look great on young Knights wall in his bedroom. A fish cut out would look great on the wall with a hook, line and sinker made of steel.

Punches

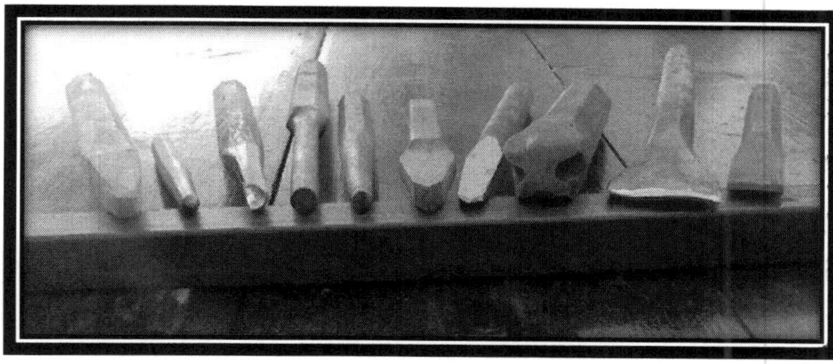

After you have gotten use to using the fire and your hand tools you may find making your own tools a great joy. The round punch is one of the easiest tools to make. You could start with mild steel if that is all you have, but if you can find a coil spring from a car or truck at an auto repair shop or junk yard this would be better. Heat and straighten out a couple of feet of the round spring. Cut to about 10" and reheat the whole thing then cover it with sand or dirt or ash and allow to cool. This is called annealing and it will make a better tool. Heat and shape with your hammer one end to be square and tapered. Then work it into an octagon, then back to round. Dress the two ends. The end that will receives the hammer blow should be squared off and the edges ground to a 45 degree angle. All of the tool should be free of burrs and cracks. These little imperfections could cause a chip to break off and fly into your eye or that of a spectators. A belt sander is a great way to finish this tool off. You could start with a heavy grit and work it down to a fine and have a near chrome looking tool. Shinny tools are good to look at but not any more effective in the shop.

If you are making a specialty punch like the eye set

punch, start with the round tapered punch you just made above and heat the tip to a light red to yellow heat. Hold it over a BB size ball bearing and strike the other end. This will create a concave impression on the tip. In order to get this done and not shoot your ball bearing across the shop, first make a small divot in a plate of steel with the tip of a drill bit. Set your ball bearing in it and save yourself a lot of time and trouble searching for it on the floor. When done you may have to use file, grinder or sander to make the walls even around the newly formed eye set, re-temper the point and you are ready to go. This is the same process to make a rivet set.

Drift Punch

The big difference in a drift punch compared to others is that the drift has its thickest point in the middle of the shaft. It starts a the working point tapering up to its thickest point then tapers down a little to the striking end. This allows the drift punch to widen out a hole then drops through the work and out the bottom of the hardy hole.

To make a drift punch first select a good quality piece of steel. A ½ inch round piece of tool steel, an old punch, or a length of an old coil spring. Straiten and prepare it as best you can. Hammer 2/3 of the shaft square and continue the square as a taper down to the size of a point that you want. Shape the other end with a less dramatic tapper ending with a larger striking end.

The Drift can be left as a square or round depending on what is needed.

At the End of the Day

After a long day of hammering, bending and stoking of the coal fire, one is covered with soot, slag and iron rust. It never fails that when I blow my nose it produces a lot of black output. That is what your nose is made to do, catch the dust in the air and keep it out of our lungs. I try but, it is almost impossible to stay out of the smoke completely. I have found a couple of tricks to clear things out.

- Hot Peppers. Eat jalapenos in some dish or salsa on chips or if you are in need of a little more help there is the habanero. This never fails to make my nose run and then I clear out a lot of crud.
- Swimming. Spending time in the water is seasonal unless you can go to a gym. This exercises your lungs and everything else. The moist air and the extra gulps of water that you get will help clean out your lungs.
- In really bad cases, ask your Doctor if using an expectorant would be right for you. It would loosen up the mucus and with deep breaths and coughs will force the dust particles out.

Grandpa Arthur Tuttle's Forge

Railroad spike Gnomes. Sold for $25.00 ea. They are sitting on my Wee Smithy anvil (seen on pg. 59) with the little blower in front.

Finishing Steel

Clean Up

Forging steel always leaves a flaky charcoal gray surface on the work. To remove this use a steel wire hand brush or wire wheel.

Bee's Wax

Years ago before the invention of spray paint cans the village smithy would apply a coat of bee's wax to the metal while it was still warm. This would melt and coat the new product preserving it until it was shipped upstream, out west or purchased at the local hardware store. Wax can be bought on the net at www.omahavillagesmithy.com or find a local bee keeper and barter with him. You could go out and find a bee's nest and extract some yourself, but that is a little more risky.

Varnish

You could just go buy a can from your local hardware store but that isn't as fun as making it yourself. Making varnish the old fashion way is done with bee's wax, rosin from pine trees and turpentine. Bee's wax is easily obtainable, turpentine you can buy from most hardware stores, and rosin can be bought off the internet or just walk out in to the park and look for tree branches that have been broken or cut off and obtain some.

Collecting the pine sap.

Bring a large soup can and a knife or scraper. Look for the old whitish dribble from wounds in the tree. Scrape it off and put into a can. You will need to collect about 2 cups of sap to make one cup of resin. Resin is just the cleaned and boiled down form of tree sap. A small step ladder may help as you reach for the prizes in the forest. When you get back home slowly warm this up and best do it out side. When totally liquefied pour it through the finest screen you can find. Window screen will do for the first run. This will get out all of the wood chips and bugs. Follow up by reheating and pouring it through a tea strainer or any finer metal screen.

Turpentine is a by-product of making rosin. If you could capture the vapors you wouldn't have to buy any turpentine. This being said, don't worry about cooking down the resin to a hard rosin. You will be reconstituting it back in the next step. If you want to make Rosin then continue to cook it down until it is very thick and pour it in a metal pan. As it cools score it with a knife making 1 inch cubes. If you make it hard enough it could be used for rosining up your bow, so you can play the fiddle on a Saturday night.

In a double boiler, again you should do this outside for safety, add into a large enamel pot;

Varnish Recipe

- 1 cup rosin,
- 1 cup bee's wax,
- 3 cups turpentine

Heat until dissolved into a harmonious liquid. The product should cool to a pourable liquid and if it thickens on the shelf between uses just add more turpentine. You may need to reheat.

When using, apply to clean dry iron work after it is cool and has been brushed. This varnish will give your work a rich satiny sheen. It is great to use in conjunction with the brass patina.

Brass Patina

The warm glow of brass is always inviting and adds

an antique look to your work. If you want the brass patina, use a steel brush and clean the work.

Heat to about 400 degrees, (which is still in the black heat range), then while hot brush with a clean brass wire. Brush lightly to apply high lights on highest points, pushing harder will give you the brass coating deeper into the detail of your work. Then fix the look by applying a top coat of clear varnish, or enamel.

Heat Bluing

To get a simple blued finish brush your work clean, and slowly heat over a fire not in the fire as you did when forging it. As the temperature raises the color of the clean metal with change. You can choose to stop at a straw color, light blue or dark blue. When your work is at the color you want quench it in oil (cooking oil, motor oil) and allow to cool. The oil adds carbon to the surface of to work creating a fine barrier layer of protective coating. Wipe clean and apply clean oil or use a solvent to remove oil then coat with lacquer or clear enamel.

Accent Painting

Spraying on clear enamel will give you a traditional look of charcoal gray but if you want to take it up a notch try mixing color paint of the same brand with the clear. Spray it into a paper cup to mix, then applied with a brush, sponge or cloth. You will get the base color of charcoal gray from the metal plus accent color but it shouldn't look like it was heavily brushed on. If you have the fund or otherwise have access to lacquer paints called candy colors you can use these without the base coats to achieve the same effect.

Glossary of Terms

Anvil. A large mass of steel on which heated steel or iron is worked into shapes.

Anneal. Steel heated to an even critical heat, in the light red range, then is allowed to cool slowly to soften the metal before working.

Ash dump. A levered trap door on the bottom of the fire pot used to clear airway to the fire from the blower. A bucket is placed under it to receive the hot ashes through the bottom of the forge.

Ball-peen hammer. Refers to the semi spherical ball on one end of the hammer head. It is used in moving metal in all directions and in adding texture to the final product.

Babbitt A soft cast-able metal used in old machinery as bearing material. Babbitt came in a lead base and other combinations of metals like tin, copper, and antimony.

Bellows. An old piece of equipment that could be made by a smith from common materials. The two-chambered forge bellows is the most common type of bellows used by blacksmiths for delivering near constant flow of air to the forge.

Blacksmith The person working with iron and steel. So named for the black oxidization or slag on the metal after it cools

.

Bloomery A furnace used to smelt iron ore and producing a bloom or lump of crude iron which then is worked into wrought iron and higher grades of iron and steel.

Borax also known as sodium borate, is used in laundering of clothes. Borax has many uses but for the blacksmith it is used as a flux. It lowers the melting point of the unwanted iron oxide (*scale*), allowing it to run off during forge welding.

Brazing Using brass or bronze to join steel and iron together.

Briquettes Pressed saw dust used in cooking on the grill but useless on the forge.

Brine Salt water, often used for quenching and hardening hot steel, and making great pickles.

Carbon Steel is steel that has enough carbon content to harden it for use as tools.

Case Hardening Allowing your iron to absorb carbon on the surface to harden it.

Cast Iron has a carbon alloy of 2.1%. It is not malleable even when hot, but is great for casting into shapes.

Charcoal Hard wood burned with little oxygen, can be used in the forge or grill.

Clinker The impurities melted together and clumping in the bottom of the fire pot.

Coke Coal after the oils and tar have been burned out.

Chisel, Cold A cold chisel is a thick chisel used to cut metal while it is cold.

Chisel, Hot A hot chisel is a thinner bladed chisel and used to cut hot metal.

Contraction The opposite of expansion. Is a shortening movement seen when the metal is cooled off.

Die A form made to help the Smith make many copies of the same thing.

Drawing Out To thin or make the metal longer by forging. To temper steel and draw out to a particular color heat range.

Drifts Punches used to enlarge holes to a particular size.

Drill Press A wall mounted or floor based machine used to drill holes in work fixed in a holding devise.

Ductility the ability for steel to deform under tensile stress and to be stretched into a wire or some other form.

Farrier A tradesman that has branched off from his blacksmith trade and specialized in working with horses.

Ferrous, Fe++ is Iron. It is the four most common element in the world.

Fire Brick Bricks made to withstand high temperatures without breaking down or cracking.

Fire Pot is the bowl in which the coal fire is contained. Is where the air mixes with the fire and includes the ash dump.

Flatter This tool is held over the work and struck by a sledge hammer with the purpose of flattening out imperfections left in the metal from hammers.

Flue The flue is the chimney stack on the forge.

Fuller A protruding shape used to draw out metal and form it. Can be used with a top fuller or swage and hammer.

Flux A substance used in welding to reduce oxidation of heated iron or steel. Commonly is borax or a mix containing borax.

Forge A table containing an air blown fire to heat metal. Could be fueled by gas or coal.

Forge Welding The act of fusing two pieces of steel or iron together at a white heat.

Foundry The operation of melting iron and casting it into shapes.

Hammer Pitch A solid blow from a hammer should land with the face of the hammer touching uniformly across the work.

Hardness is the ability to resist wear. Is tested by the Rockwell indent method. There are several scales, each for a different material.

Hold Downs A tool that wedges into the pritchel hole or hardy and holds your work on top of the anvil.

Hardy Hardies are small additional tools that help shape metal. Some common hardies are the short, heavy chisels used to cut steel while still cold, the thin bladed ones, used for cutting hot steel. Other hardies have faces used for specialized work, such as rounding a horse shoe heel, and shaping designs into the work. Most are referred to fullers and swages.

Iron The elemental substance noted on the periodic table as Fe++ element # 26. It is named after the Latin term ferrum meaning iron. It has a carbon content lower than 0.05%.

Malleability Malleability is similar to the ductility property, it is a material's ability to be form into a thin sheet by hammering or rolling.

Mild Steel. Mild steel has replaced Wrought Iron. It is readily available and easily worked on the forge. It is not suitable for heat treating.

Metallurgy The study of metals.

Mushrooming The spreading of metal as on the end of a chisel that has been struck repeatedly. Should be removed so not to break off and injure the user or a bystander.

Patina The natural or artificial finish on an item.

Plasticity Plasticity describes the ability of a material to be shaped as in hammering heated steel in a new form without cracking, chipping or otherwise failing.

Punch A tool used in shaping or pushing through or marking metal.

Peen Is the shaped face of the hammer such as the ball, straight, cross, diagonal peen.

Pritchel Hole The round hole in the tail of the anvil. Used for punching through metal and for hold down tools.

Slack Tub A tub, bucket or barrel of water used to cool off the hot metal.

Slag is the scale that flakes off while cooling during working the metal or when plunging it into the water.

Smithy The building in which the blacksmith works.

Smith The Smith is a shortened form of blacksmith, referring to the person.

Steel An alloy of carbon in iron makes steel. The amount of carbon determines the hardness of the steel. Steel has a small amount of carbon, ranging from between 0.002% and 2.1%

by weight.

Spring Steel Steel with a high carbon content giving it the ability to bend and return to its original position as in coil springs and leaf springs.

Swage A hardy tool with a concave surface or inside shape to aid in forming of metal.

Swage Block A heavy steel or cast iron block with multiple shapes on all surfaces. Is used to shape metal uniformly.

Stainless Steel is an alloy metal with a minimum of 10.5% chromium.

Tang the end of a tool that receives a handle, such as a knife, sword or file.

Tensile strength is the maximum stress that a material can withstand while being stretched or pulled before failing or breaking.

Trip Hammer a machine that delivers hammer blows repeatedly.

Tuyere is the diffusing plate that sits on top of the air inlet in the fire pot. It allows air to be broke up into many streams and keeps the coals from falling into the ash dump.

Wrought Iron. Wrought iron is made with a very low carbon content 0.1 to 0.25%. It still has impurities of slag in it that when worked with gives a wood grain look to the metal. Wrought iron has been replace for the most part with mild steel.

Upset The act of upsetting steel is to thicken it by hammering it into itself and creating a thicker mass of metal.

Vise An anchored device that clamps your project and holds it so it can be worked on.

About the Author

Looking back in our genealogy, I have found that I can claim to be a fourth generation blacksmith.

Great Grand Dad and Grandpa Art Tuttle were working Smiths. Father was a modern equivalent, a welder in a small shop. My brother and I worked in manufacturing as welders. We learned to work with stainless steel, aluminum, as well as black iron. When I was about 18 years of age my father gave me my first blacksmithing tools. He blessed me with grandfather's forge, anvil and a bucket of small hand tools. Over the years I have honed my skills, collected and made other tools to work with. I have enjoyed practicing this craft and sharing it with others through demonstrations and books.